RESOLVING PROBLEM PATTERNS

with Clean Language and Autogenic Metaphor

Wayfinder Press
London, England

ISBN 978-0-9561607-5-1

All enquiries to info@wayfinderpress.co.uk

*How can client patterns be discerned, decoded,
and the information within them be released?**

*Introduction by Clean Language creator David Grove
to a research seminar in London November 1999

Contents

Preface

At a time when psychoactive drugs are being prescribed more widely than at any time in history, it is more important than ever to educate ourselves about the alternatives. The latest revisions to the psychiatric diagnostic manual extend its remit to include 'generalised anxiety disorder', laying the everyday sadnesses and frustrations of life open to diagnosis and medication as mental illnesses. It is questionable whether the average fifteen-minute diagnostic session with a psychiatrist or seven minutes with a general practitioner is enough for the effective detection and determination of tangled patterns of addiction, anxiety, inadequacy, grief, fear, depression and so on. The tranquilisers and anti-depressants prescribed for these common conditions have frequently been authorized for use on the flimsiest of evidence, they expose patients to side effects and dependency problems, and they won't come within a mile of the underlying cause.[1]

The drug-free resolution of problem patterns of behaviour, feeling, and belief is as important for health professionals to support as it is for their patients and clients to achieve. Otherwise we all circle endlessly, helplessly reiterating the unproductive patterns of the past. This guide has a bias towards the talking therapies – and in particular the radical new art and science of Clean Language – but its precepts and procedures are applicable to any area of human enquiry, so you might allow the words 'therapist' or 'facilitator' in the text to act as metaphor for doctor, researcher, teacher, coach, counsellor, manager, parent, or any agent of change you wish. We are all therapists or facilitators of one kind or another.

In most of the excerpts from Clean Language process that appear here, the full syntax has been abbreviated. The complete Clean Language syntax is repetitive – a necessary (and irresistible) pattern in a therapeutic or facilitative context, but a bit tedious to read. The full syntax and a complete set of Clean questions are set out, explained, and explored in the book *TRUST ME, I'M THE PATIENT: Clean Language, Metaphor, and the New Psychology of Change* (Wayfinder Press 2012).

---

1 For a devastating critique of pharmaceutical research and approval procedures, see *Bad Pharma*, Dr. Ben Goldacre (Fourth Estate 2012).

Introduction

We do not seek out a therapist or facilitator because we have a problem. We go because we realize – often after years of private struggle – that without intervention, the repetitive nature of certain thoughts, feelings, or behaviours will continue into the future. We notice a pattern to our lives or relationships that we do not like, but do not know how to change. Indeed, we might be quite reluctant to change, because there is a tremendous need in most of us for continuity and consistency. Even if our patterns of anxiety, addiction, grief, or fear are disruptive or disabling, we will go to a great deal of trouble to hang on to them.

Traditional psychotherapy, coaching, teaching, and interviewing have a history of imposing external patterns (the therapist's/ coach's/teacher's/interviewer's) onto internal experience (the patient's/client's/student's/interviewee's). Is it any wonder that suspects in police custody later retract confessions made under the influence of their interrogators, that patients in long-term analysis take so long to learn not to need analysis, and that clients for drug therapy or short-term cognitive-behavioural therapy tend to relapse? One of the considerable benefits of working in Clean Language and Autogenic Metaphor is that complex disabling patterns can be codified into relatively simple configurations which can be explored by the client without shape-changing interference by the facilitator. A problem pattern can be more efficiently discerned, more easily decoded, and more effectively resolved.

Clean Language is a minimalist methodology of questioning that facilitates the client to self-model (make sense of) their problem patterns at the threshold of consciousness, the place where self-knowledge connects to original source, the place where change can be explored and matured.

Autogenic (Therapeutic) Metaphor is self-information generated spontaneously by the client untainted by therapist prescription or suggestion. It is a precious container for retrieving information from the unconscious in a pure and accessible form.

Compare "I'm so depressed I don't know what to do" with its metaphorical equivalent "It's like I'm on a roller-coaster." A roller-coaster can stop and the passengers can get off, or the track can level out and become a railway going somewhere. There are a multitude of options available in the metaphor that are unavailable in the conceptual word 'depressed'.

Penny Tompkins and James Lawley[1]

My purpose in this five-part paper is to help you identify problem patterns and to consider how best to facilitate your clients and colleagues – and, indeed, yourself – to discern, decode, and resolve them.

> Part I   What is a pattern?
> Part II   How can patterns be discerned?
> Part III How can problem patterns be decoded?
> Part IV What happens when the information within
>   is released?
> Part V   Then what happens?

I shall propose that our traditional ways of attempting to resolve problem patterns – in effect from outside or alongside the pattern – are redundant, and in their place offer a method of exploring and resolving them *from within the pattern itself*.

₪

Note

1 All Lawley & Tompkins quotations are from *Metaphors in Mind: Transformation through Symbolic Modelling* (Developing Company Press 2000).

Part I
What Is A Pattern?

Like the circles that you find
In the windmills of your mind.
Alan & Marilyn Bergman

When we get stuck, we get stuck in a repetitive pattern of behaviour, beliefs, or mind-games over which we feel we have little or no control.

Patterns in space, time, and form

My client Colin is a thoughtful, intelligent, 40-something teacher. He sits carefully, hands folded, and smiles at me. Well, I'm interpreting his tight little, minimal, almost painful stretching of the lips as a smile, but I could be wrong. "I've been going round in circles for years," he says.

Figure 1 A metaphor in space, time and form

I [form]
have been [time]
going round [space and form]
in circles [form]
for years [time]

Of course, Colin might not care very much whether his pattern is in space, time, or Camembert cheese. All he knows is that he is stuck, confused, and needs help. The more I know about patterns, the better I'll be able to help clients like Colin know themselves better and become more the kind of people they want to be.

Space, time, and form have been around since they were created in the big bang some 15 billion years ago, so it's time we got to know them better, particularly in the context of therapeutic enquiry. They are the media in which all patterns manifest. A problem pattern might appear in space, or time, or form, or in a combination of all three. Colin's metaphor of going round in circles for years has the form of 'circles', the time element of 'years', and the spatial location (because everything has to be somewhere) of 'going round'. There is likely to be vital information in every part of this pattern: the number of years, the circumference of the circles, the whereabouts of going round, the view en route, what happened just before the pattern began, and so on.

The components of this metaphor have not been randomly chosen by Colin's unconscious. Each item will carry symbolic significance in his psychopathology and contain clues for resolving the problem they represent.

Not all patterns will take our attention in the same way as Colin's. What patterns are you aware of as you read this? The regularity of the margins on the page (a spatial pattern)? The consistent use of Century Schoolbook as the font (a pattern of form)? And if your sensory acuity is particularly acute today, you might have noticed a sequence of three interrogative sentences one after the other (a pattern of form in space over time).

Distinguishing pattern

What distinguishes pattern from non-pattern, or randomness, or just something else? Can a single vertical line be a pattern?

In a client's written statement, it might symbolise the 'I' of the client (a massive metaphysical pattern in itself). In a drawn metaphor landscape, it might represent a longitude or the cosmic axis (geodetic patterns); a path to the future or a dividing line between left and right (graphical patterns); and many other things.

A single horizontal line could represent the horizon, a facial expression, an 'm-dash' connecting two ideas, an underline, the concept of separation, subtraction, etc.

$+$

A combination of | and − could stand for a mathematical operation, an affirmative preposition, a physical intersection, and so on. A single symbol can represent a multitude of possible configurations of space, time, and form. The hieroglyphic below could hold the whole of a client's experience.

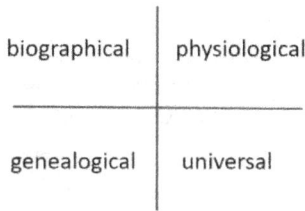

biographical	physiological
genealogical	universal

Figure 2 Client information quadrants[1]

What distinguishes pattern from non-pattern is organisational coherence and continuity. Is it any wonder that even though we might be desperate for change we keep on repeating the same old patterns for years? Coherence and continuity are powerful anchors.

Defining pattern

One English dictionary defines pattern as *a configuration or grouping of parts or elements with a coherent structure.*

The word *configuration* means both 'outline' and 'arrangement'. An outline is an economical representation of the fullness of what it configures. An arrangement refers to two or more things in relationship. A problem pattern could appear either in outline form ("I'm not feeling too good about myself") or in some sort of arrangement of parts. These might be reasonably coherent and accessible ("I'm stuck in this dark corner") or less so ("I've been told I'm aggressive and abusive and I almost feel the need to be").

Systems theorist Fritjof Capra called pattern

A configuration of ordered relationships

but I believe a configuration *is* an ordered relationship, whether the order is apparent or not. In terms of problem patterns, it is often not apparent. Nice word, configuration. We'll keep it.

The words *parts* and *elements*, however, we can do without. One part or element might represent many more, as we have seen. Thus, a single symbol in a client's metaphor might be a component of a pattern or a pattern in itself. The concept of 'parts or elements' is subsumed in 'configuration'. We can simplify our definition to *A configuration with a coherent structure.*

However, just as a building is made up of many components, the structure of a problem is constructed of more than one part. 'Configuration with structure' is tautological. Lose 'structure'. That leaves us with *A configuration with coherence.* You could argue that the word *coherence* ('a natural or reasonable connection') is pretty meaningless in the context of what we already know about problem patterns, but we'll keep it because it draws attention to the fact that configurations in space have form. *A configuration with coherence.*

Is something missing? The notion of **pattern** normally requires a configuration to repeat. Repetition takes place in space (as in a wallpaper pattern) or time (as in the passage of the seasons). Time, whether over milliseconds or millennia, supposes some kind of continuity.

So we end up with *A configuration with coherence and continuity.*

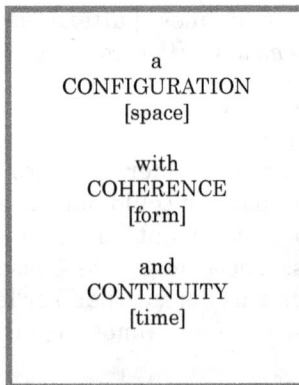

```
                a
         CONFIGURATION
            [space]

              with
          COHERENCE
            [form]

              and
          CONTINUITY
             [time]
```

Figure 3 Defining pattern

And because continuity supposes predictability, the word *pattern* becomes a metaphor for a more or less predictably repeating relationship of parts.

Problem patterns

A problem pattern is simply a pattern that gives the client problems. It could be a long-repeated behaviour, feeling, thought, or belief: "I'm depressed again," "I've always been frightened of spiders," "I can never get where I want to be." These are not monolithic constructs. They are made up of a number of interacting components and sub-structures. Their importance in the context of client facilitation is that as internalized configurations in space with coherence of form and continuity over time, *they can be elicited by the facilitator, deciphered by the client, and changed.* Their sources can be traced, their fabric examined, their conditions resolved.

₪

Note to Part I

1 Client information quadrants after David Grove's work on information domains. Present information about the client is generally available in the biographical quadrant; less apparent information in the physiological, genealogical, and universal quadrants. We can exclude the therapist's intuition or cognition as reliable sources of information about the client. They can be persuasive indicators, but if they intrude into client pattern, they are a dubious influence at best.

Grove used to imagine a gear lever at the intersection of the four quadrants, allowing the facilitator to shift into any one of four gears (information sources) with the possibility of a return into neutral and thence into another gear.

Part II
How Can Patterns Be Discerned?

Not much can be done about a pattern until it can be separated from the mass of other data that permeates and surrounds it. How can a facilitator encourage this awareness without falling into the trap of misinterpreting the information that appears? How can clients get to recognize the patterns to their unwanted behaviours and beliefs without the need to keep repeating them? Discernment requires more than simple recognition; it involves interpretation and judgement.

What do you see on the right? Two profiles? A pair of worms? The outline of a vase or balustrade? Actually, they're squiggles. You have never seen these particular squiggles before, but you interpret them the way you do because the shapes they make, or something like them, are already in your brain.

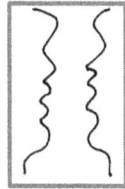

Which is why you recognize them. Literally, re – cognize, know them again, you are re–minded. Were you able to see two people kissing a vase perfectly formed to their faces? Or two people head butting a large balloon? Less easily, I dare say, because it is unlikely you would have had these images already in your brain. Until now. The chances are that in future you will recognize two people head-butting a balloon with ease.

Seeing (hearing, tasting, etc.) and *recognition* are related but unalike events. They are not to be compared. We need to take a further conceptual step between *recognition* and *judgement*. What happens in the brain after sight and before recognition, and after recognition and before judgement, is a turmoil of generalization, deletion, and distortion that the mind must manage in order to make sense of what would otherwise be an overwhelming onslaught of meaningless sensory data.

Discernment thus involves choice. There are so many choices to be made every micro-moment of our lives that almost all of them have to be made unconsciously. The reality that emerges from this process is tenuous and often ambiguous, because of the common associations the bodybrain makes – and cannot help but make – to its sensory input.

Associative patterning

Memories, we know from a wealth of scientific research and our own experience, are rarely immutable. They change over time and take their shape from the needs of the present. Every memory is an act of creation. This makes associative patterning – in which sensory input from the world prompts capricious traces of memory filtered through current emotional state and present intention – a dangerous game for any therapist to play. As the brain connects present perception and the memory of something comparable, it reinforces the neural pathways between them, which increases the chances of detecting the 'same' (actually no more than a similar, often inaccurately remembered) pattern in future.

There is a sound evolutionary rationale for our need to conjure up memories and make instantaneous choices:

> sabre-toothed tiger (present reality)
> + tiger jumped on companion last week (terrible memory)
> = dead companion (bad pattern)
> sequence learned: avoid these animals in future

Associative patterning helped us survive.

The more fearful or insecure we feel as facilitators about what is going on for the client, the more likely we are to interpret what we see or hear in the light of our own ravelled patterns, present and past, good and bad, real and imagined. 'Nescient anxiety syndrome', the fear of not knowing, can result in a therapist running well ahead of the client's reality: making unwarranted inferences, peddling undue influence, and needlessly, ill-advisedly affecting the outcome. As psychotherapist James Lawley has said, "There's a fine line between logical inference and self-fulfilling prophecy." If we imagine what the client means (by inferring it 'logically' from what they have said) and put this meaning to them, there is every likelihood that they will click the okay button and save it for themselves. It will become the default meaning. It will replace, obscure, dilute, or even extinguish the client's own. The therapist's conjecture becomes the client's new reality.

Consider Figure #4.

Figure 4 *Count the invisible triangles*

Actually, there are no triangles here. These are lines on a page. But notice how readily – even if not prompted with an instruction ("Count the invisible triangles") – the brain fills in the gaps between the lines to make a familiar figure. Or two, or three, or even five. The triangles we 'see' are hallucinations. The brain is filling in the missing bits from other patterns. What other patterns? Our pre-existing patterns as perceivers.

'Perception' comes from the Latin *percipere*, 'to receive'. Each of the 100-million receptor cells of the retina receives a patch of dark or light, a shade of colour, or a certain configuration of line. Transmits this data undifferentiated along the optic nerve to the brain. The brain receives these numberless impulses. Selects. Forms patterns. Compares them to patterns already present in memory. And makes subjective meaning. Our minds cannot help it. We are unstoppable makers of meaning, however objective and responsive we like to think we can be. Every image and sound we believe we see or hear has been filtered via a multiplicity of visual and auditory inputs through unavoidable mental processes of generalization, deletion, and distortion. We see and hear what we have been programmed (arguably, what we have programmed ourselves) to see and hear.

In the context of facilitating others, Clean Language can save us from ourselves. The Clean syntax succeeds in objectifying information from the client by insulating the facilitator from personal patterns, prejudices, archetypes, and stereotypes accumulated over millennia of inherited wisdom and foolishness. My Clean questioning of the client's metaphor – "What kind of circles?" "Is there anything else about going round?" – optimizes the potential for ingenerate change by identifying *with* the pattern and working not from outside or alongside, but *within* it. (There is more on how this works in Part III.)

Recovered information begins to appear as a result of the therapist's Clean questioning and the client's self-modelling. Colin begins to be aware of:

coherence (*"This is the perfect circle"*)
continuity (*"I'm going round again"*)
connection (*"My dad was the same"*)
consequence (*"I get depressed"*)
difference (*"I've never seen my stuckness this way before"*)

and a dozen other associations and relationships.

Conspicuous patterns

What do the patterns around you – the motif on the curtains, the number of cups of coffee you drink in a week, the song on the radio that is more than a random sequence of notes – have in common that make them conspicuous?

Repetition

How many events do there have to be before we are aware of something repeating?

I've been going round and round in circles for years.

Most people would agree that a pattern would be indicated if an event had occurred three times (in the example above, "round", "round", and "circles"). Note that the form of the pattern ('round', 'circles', 'cycle', 'spiral', 'carousel', 'back to where I began,' etc.) may not be exactly the same with each repetition. Both conscious and unconscious are signalling the pattern, and they will do it any way they wish.

Colin is stuck. He knows little or nothing about the configuration of his stuckness, so he is in a vulnerable state. He might like to hear what I think about his anxiety, obsession or addiction. It would be relatively easy for me to suggest that it could be the effect of this or that and that he should do X or Y. He might even go away satisfied – for a while, until the next stressful event – illness, argument, a death in the family – when the same old pattern returns. What Colin really wants is for the pattern to change. And this is the kind of resolution that can only come from within.

Implied patterns

Every therapeutic or developmental journey will reveal a landscape that has been inaccessible until that very moment. There might be no words to express the essence of the experience, or there might be words that are not quite right. It would be a foolish facilitator who dismissed the possibility of a pattern if the client were unable to describe it conveniently or coherently. We have seen how a pattern is apparent at the third repetition, but what about two events – the original plus one – indicating a third? If we notice someone walking briskly by and see them long enough to register they have taken two paces, we can reasonably infer the third. If we hear two notes on the piano, we can readily hypothesize a third that will produce a certain melody.

I've been going round and round ...

A facilitator must be prepared to be wrong, but normally it only takes two events to establish a pattern: the original plus one. In music, 'repetition' is a passage performed a second time. Which brings us back to the intriguing question, can patterns come in ones?

I've been going round and ...

Patterns in metaphor

We have already seen how the simplest of graphic images can contain a whole world. Does the same hold for words?

There's like a wall around me.

I hear a record of rejection playing in my head.

A single phrase – "a wall around me", "a record of rejection" – could carry the entire history of a client's psychopathology. The Greeks had a word for it. *Meta*, 'change' + *phora*, 'carry' = *metaphor*, meaning 'transfer' or 'carry' across.

Figure 5 Metaphor: the Greeks had a word for it

Metaphor is a higher-level container for conveying information across the (metaphorical) threshold between the unconscious and conscious minds. It originates in the unconscious and becomes manifest – verbally or nonverbally characterized – in consciousness. This remarkable phenomenon enables therapist and client to work directly at the place where self-knowledge connects to original source, where unconsciously generated change will be recognized, specified, felt, and reinforced. Whether the pattern is conspicuous or inferred, plain or deeply disguised, common or complex, autogenic metaphor carries information from the deep reaches of the ocean to an accessible shore where its characteristics are more readily discerned and appraised.

> Therapist And when you're hopelessly confused, that's hopelessly confused like what?
>
> *Client Like I'm going round in circles.*
>
> Therapist And like you're going round in circles. And when going round in circles, how many circles?
>
> *Client Three. One like a massive traffic jam on the North Circular. A smaller one that's a dirty-looking pond. And the third is a helicopter in ever-decreasing circles running out of fuel.*

In two Clean questions, the client has gone from "hopelessly confused" to a situation that might still be difficult to unravel, but has latent resources for resolving the problem. A traffic jam can clear and the traffic run smoothly; a pond can be drained or have hidden depths; a helicopter can be refuelled and flown up to provide an overview. Almost all problem patterns contain the nucleus of their resolution. It depends on how the pattern is perceived.

Perceiving pattern

A great deal of what is interesting about patterns revolves round our perception of them. All patterns require a perceiver and all perception involves patterning. Even in the case of the simplest possible indicator, a dot representing a single point of light, say ...

•

... there is a pattern in that we distinguish the point of light only in relation to the lack-of-light or less-light surrounding it. If we place our attention on the dot, we might see it as having form or structure and appearing to be in front of the background. The ground can be seen as relatively homogenous and extending behind and beyond the dot. But what precisely is the 'pattern' this creates? Must it repeat before it may be said to be a pattern?

• • • •

What if on closer inspection each dot turns out to be a potential pattern in itself?

☺ ☻ ☻ ☼

Or if it repeats oddly?

• • • •

• • • •

You might say to your client the equivalent of "I notice that one line of your dots is higher than the other" and congratulate yourself on your objectivity. Well, think again. 'Line', 'dots', 'your', and 'higher' are your metaphors. The client might respond, "Actually the first point of light represents the world in space as seen from the Mars, the next is the town where I live, and the others represent the concept that every apparently single entity is made up of many parts, and I am seeing these from several perceptual positions, not from one as you seem to be, although now that you have drawn my attention to your perception, I find myself thinking you could be right, I am not the expert, my perceptions must be wrong in some way and now I'm even more confused."

And let us say that as your facilitator I make no observation at all about what I imagine to be your pattern, but simply draw your attention to it.

> And is there anything else about .. ['that' or gesture to the drawing] ..?
>
> *Yes. They make a sequence.*

Will you now be any wiser about your pattern? Probably. A more accessible configuration ("sequence") has appeared in your here and now narrative. To help you familiarize yourself with your sequence, I might ask

> And when they make a sequence, what is the first thing that happens? ... And what happens next? ... And then what happens?

Patterns can be perceived in four inter-related ways:

1 by focusing on the foreground
2 by bringing up the background
3 by attending to the relationship between foreground and background, and
4 by following indirect indicators.

1 Focusing on the foreground

A facilitator must constantly make choices about where to direct the client's attention. There is no shortage of possibility. Every client presents an abundance of foreground, background, and indirect information. In the foreground is immediate 'here and now' data (see the biographical quadrant on page 11). The client's body language on entering the room, their choice of where to sit, the narrative they bring to the session, and so on. In one way or another, the client is already manifesting the problem that brings them to you. They cannot not. The pattern is present.

Clean Language makes the most of this not necessarily evident fact by requiring the therapist to address a substantive verbal or nonverbal item presented by the client rather than one arising from the therapist's own speculation, assumption, or colouring of the item ("I notice you seem anxious," etc.).

> Colin *I'm going round in circles.*
>
> Therapist [has no idea what the client is talking about] And you're going round in circles. And when going round in circles, what kind of circles could those circles be?
>
> Colin *I keep on making the same mistakes.*

The client has responded conceptually. The obvious Clean foreground question now would be 'What kind of mistakes?' though that could provoke an outpouring of content, a recital of all the mistakes Colin ever made, rather than holding him in process. A specifically pattern-related choice would be, 'And when you keep on making the same mistakes, is there anything else about that 'same'? In this case, the therapist invites the original metaphor to return or a new one to appear:

> That is keep on making the same mistakes like what?
>
> *Like sowing seeds in the same barren ground.*

Foreground choices are now between the symbolic 'sowing', 'seeds', and 'barren ground' – any of which could have fruitful possibilities.

The client's words and inflexions are perhaps the most revealing of all foreground figures, in the sense that every word, every inflexion, every space between words has a contribution to make beyond its common or conversational meaning. How can I help Colin discern the underlying pattern that gives coherence and continuity to this assortment of mini-metaphors ('sowing', 'seeds', 'barren', 'ground')? He might discover more depth to these two-dimensional figures by continuing to focus on the foreground until more components of the pattern emerge ... or we might shift his attention to the background.

2 Bringing up the background

There are two meanings to 'background' we can work with here – one spatial and structural (as in the background setting to foreground components of the metaphor landscape), the other temporal and sequential (as in the background history of the client or a background perspective on events).

> And when sowing seeds in the same barren ground, where could that barren ground come from?
>
> *From vicious circles of deprivation.*

Background information becomes available to the client from physiological and genealogical sources – bodymind memories of life events; family, cultural and environmental history; acquired beliefs, values, and such.

Colin now has a sequence that connects his original 'going round in circles' (foreground) via 'sowing seeds in barren ground' (foreground shading into background) to 'vicious circles of deprivation' (likely background). Is there more to this metaphor?

> And where could those vicious circles of deprivation come from?

Depending on your preferred model of therapy, you might speculate that they came from an unhappy childhood, lines of negative energy, or being kidnapped by aliens. In this case:

> *From my stomach. From a reel of cotton wound in knots.*

> And from your stomach, from a reel of cotton wound in knots.
> And when reel of cotton wound in knots [decides to invite the

client to move time further back] what happens just before wound in knots?

Everything is going smoothly.

The implication here is that something happened that resulted in reel of cotton being wound in knots rather than everything going smoothly. Questioning the background provenance of the circles happened to bring up the knots, a classic container for trauma, and established a sequence to the pattern.

And everything is going smoothly. [Draws client's attention to the sequence so far.] And when going smoothly, and then reel of cotton wound in knots [decides to invite client to move time further forward, drawing attention to the continuing development of the sequence], then what happens?

I feel confused.

This might seem like hauling the client back to where he began – going round in circles confused – but is congruent with the recurring nature of the pattern. I have honoured Colin's strategy for constructing confusion and now it is more available to him. Notice that there is no hint yet of the client decoding the pattern (Part III), only of beginning to discern it from a jumble of other data and his sense of the relationship between its various components.

3 Attending to the relationship between foreground and background

And when going smoothly, then reel of cotton wound in knots, then confused .. [lots of choice here, decides to go for a connection question] .. what is the relationship between going smoothly [background stuff] and going round in circles [original foreground]?

I'm not sure. It's to do with whoever is winding the knots.

Is this a piece of the jigsaw or a gap waiting to be filled? If the client is searching for a missing piece to the puzzle, the gap in the puzzle will have a pattern that corresponds to the missing piece. The gap creates a relationship to the piece, just as the piece creates a relationship to the gap. What is there relates to what is not there, and vice versa.

Place your attention on the background space around this foreground dot.[1]

•

Notice how the boundary between dot and background that formerly belonged to the dot alone now belongs to the dot and space in relationship. The figure-ground gives form to the figure and vice versa. All pattern is an arrangement of relationships between relationships. "It's like darning a sock," says therapist Frances Prestidge. "You have the edge of the hole, you bring threads across the hole, and they relate to each other to complete the w/hole." The pattern of the darn exists by dint of an arrangement between foreground threads, background sock, and the hole that connects them!

4 Following indirect indicators

We have focussed on the visible/audible foreground, brought up the barely-observable/faintly-heard background, and explored the relationships between them. But the configuration of the pattern is not yet discernible and the client is still confused. What else can we do?

Creator of Clean Language David Grove emphasized the value of 'tacit knowledge' – knowledge we don't know we know until it pops into consciousness. How can we learn to recognize these pointers to unconscious patterns? They are often difficult to spot, but the signs can be learnt. Here are four kinds to listen and look out for:

> *inconsequentials* – items of easy-to-miss information
> *incongruities* – mismatches between information components
> *phonetic ambiguities* – words with more than one meaning
> *nonverbal indicators* – gestures, sounds, etc.

Inconsequentials
are easily overlooked. It can take the client time to trust the therapist, or their own process, or the way information sometimes pops into consciousness without warning. Both therapist and client might be inclined to dismiss a fragment that appears in response to questioning if the fragment seems trivial, is anomalous, or appears out of nowhere. This is especially so if the client does not quite have the words, or the words are not quite right, to describe the experience.

> *Oh, it's nothing ... some sort of ... I dunno.*

And it's nothing, some sort of, you dunno. And when it's nothing, some sort of, you dunno ... is there anything else about that?

That's funny, I got a flash of a roundabout.

And a flash of a roundabout. And is there anything else about that flash of a roundabout?

This is silly. I had an image of a children's roundabout I went on when I was about three. (Pause) I was scared.

And where is that scared? ... Does it have a size or shape? ... [etc.]

Incongruities
are mismatches between component parts of the client's information. In 1905, Percival Lowell studied the movement of Uranus and Neptune around the sun and detected a slight wobble in their orbits. He believed that the inconsistency was due to the presence of another celestial body, which the telescopes of the day could not see. In 1930, his prediction came true when Pluto was discovered.

> *It's a roundabout that moves all over the place and I can't get off.*

Is there something here that is inconsistent, incongruous, or illogical? Well, roundabouts are normally to be found in one place, though Colin's could belong to a travelling fair. And if you wait long enough, a roundabout will generally stop, which will enable you to get off unless something or someone is preventing you. Every assumption we make about meaning should be held lightly and subject to constant review.

We know that the unconscious can detect patterns before the conscious mind is aware of them.[2] We might sense something unusual in a client's linguistic construction that we cannot quite make sense of, yet feel moved to explore further.

> And when it's a roundabout that moves 'all over the place' ..

> *It's one that flies, of course!*

A reminder that the metaphor landscape is not subject to everyday rules of realism. Metaphors, like dreams, have a logic of their own.

Gently drawing attention to an incongruity can lead to new information. It is (at the least) a way of clearing up ambiguity.

Phonetic ambiguities

Homophones are words with the same sound, but different meanings or spellings. The adjective 'new' and the past tense 'knew' are homophones of each other.

Homonyms are words with the same sound and spelling, but different meanings. The noun 'a bear' and the verb 'to bear' are homonyms of each other.

Homographs are words having the same spelling, but different meanings or pronunciations. The noun 'a record' and the verb 'to record' are homographs of each other.

Return for a moment to Colin's "sowing seeds". There is an improbable, though not inconceivable, homophone – 'sewing' – lurking there. Notice also that the word 'wound' in "wound in knots" (pages. 23-24) is a homograph, another potential indicator to unconscious pattern. The word "k/nots" is another. These can all be nice little signals, but our antennae need to be well tuned to detect them.

We should not assume that every ambiguity holds a relevant secondary meaning or that the additional meaning, if there is one, is ours to divine. If a client utters the word "right", we might assume they mean 'correct' or 'privilege' rather than 'okay', 'not left', 'write', etc. Having identified a potential ambiguity, we have a choice: to assume one of its possible meanings and hope to be lucky (at the risk of guessing wrongly and distorting the exchange); or to design a Clean question that retains the ambiguity while freeing the client to make explicit any meaning they choose.

> And right. And when rite, what kind of write could that wright be?

Of course, the client might have come up with a pun, a double meaning, or a homophone because they couldn't stop themselves meaning two conflicting things at once. And there might be a pattern in that.

> *It's a round, uh, circle ...*

Is the client saying 'around a circle', 'a rounder circle' or hesitating in the middle of 'a round circle'? These could all be signposts to different destinations.

And it's a round uh circle. [Therapist slurs the words slightly to leave the possibilities open] And when it's a round uh circle, is there anything else about that a round uh circle?

(Client mumbles) Yes, it's rounder than the other circle.

And it's rounder than the other ...

No, I said it surrounds the other circle, so I can't get out!

Inflections are modulations of tone or pitch that serve the linguistic function of differentiating meaning. They are full of traps for the unwary. A North American "can't" can sound indistinguishable to other ears from 'can'. An Irish "those" can be mistaken for 'doze'. A client's "lighthouse keeper" can become a 'light housekeeper' in the mind of the therapist who likes to keep things tidy. We hear one version of the client's intonation and miss the hint of a pattern in the other.

Try saying these two sentences out loud.

He was, not surprisingly, killed by the bullet.
He was not, surprisingly, killed by the bullet.

The smallest of pauses, inflexions, or hesitations can make a big difference, so we need to stay tuned.

Nonverbal indicators
A facilitator concentrating only on language might miss a key move. A wave, a gesture, an eye-shift, the angle of an elbow or foot while the client is speaking could all be (literal) pointers to unconscious patterns. There might be a tell-tale 'um', a faint smile, the raising of an eyebrow, a shrug, a widening of the eyes. If the unconscious or unspoken information these carry has been long obscured or is deeply stored, it is unlikely to appear with a fanfare.

Nonverbals usually augment the client's narrative, but they can be at odds with it, which will itself be an indicator. It takes some sensitivity backed by a certain bloody-mindedness on the part of a facilitator to pick up on indirect indicators to unconscious patterns and go with them. Here is Colin again, with a couple of inconsequentials, a nonverbal, and a phonetic ambiguity in the space of a few seconds:

Oh! A sort of, well .. (gestures) .. oh, I .. no .. it's nothing.

Most of us would be expected to follow the normal rules of rapport at this point and move on, but in Clean Language process the attention of the listener is as much on the information the client presents as it is on the client.

> *Oh!* [surprise inconsequential – did something just 'pop up'?]
>
> *A sort of, well* ... ['not-quite-the-words' – new information?]
>
> *(gesture)* [non-verbal indicator – what does it represent?]
>
> *oh, I* ... [hesitation – something unexpressed?]
>
> *no* ... [homophone of 'know' – what might he know here?]
>
> *it's nothing* [dismissive inconsequential – you can bet it's something]

Whether we pick up on conspicuous or implied patterns, focus on the foreground, bring up the background, or follow any one of a number of indirect indicators, we need simply to concentrate on what is there. There is the pattern. In one way or another, the client cannot help but express it. And as long as the facilitator stays true to Clean questioning,[3] the pattern cannot help but emerge.

In Parts I and II, we considered what patterns are and how they can be discerned. We looked at how working with Clean Language and Autogenic Metaphor minimizes interference in the processing of client information and facilitates the early stages of self-exploration.

Parts III, IV, and V describe how problem patterns once detected are decoded and explain what happens when the information within them is released. What are the key differences between what we might call 'clean' and 'unclean' approaches to facilitation?

₪

Notes to Part II

1 'Foreground' dot on 'background' expanse: note that the pattern this creates might be seen the other way round, i.e. the dot could be viewed by the client as background blackness appearing though a tiny hole in foreground whiteness. Here the facilitator goes with the more likely interpretation, but will allow for all other options until the client confirms or updates the information.

2 How the unconscious recognizes and acts on signals before the conscious mind becomes aware of them, if it ever does: Joseph Ledoux, *The Emotional Brain* (1998).

3 A definitive list of 100 Clean Language, Clean Space, and Emergent Knowledge questions can be found in Appendix C of the Clean Language book, *Trust Me, I'm The Patient*, op. cit.

Part III

How Can Problem Patterns Be Decoded?

deciphered / unscrambled / figured out[1]

Here we reflect on different ways of facilitating clients to decode their problem patterns.

You will find more emphasis on the use of Clean Language and Autogenic Metaphor. *Clean Language*, you will recall, is a minimalist intervention methodology which allows the client to self-model their own process at the threshold of consciousness, the very place that change can be facilitated and matured. *Metaphor* is a container for concentrating what would otherwise be an excess of information from the unconscious into a readily accessible form. *Autogenic* metaphor is metaphor generated spontaneously by the client untainted by therapist assumption, suggestion, or interpretation.

Parts I and II considered two questions: 'What is a pattern?' and 'How can patterns be discerned?' A repeated behaviour, feeling, thought, or belief was described in terms of a configuration in the client's internal landscape with coherence and continuity. A problem pattern is simply a pattern that gives the client problems. Two principal kinds of discernment were identified: associative (closed) discernment based on guesswork, where the therapist fills in 'missing' bits of client information from patterns of their own; and non-assumptive (open) discernment based on Clean Language questioning, where the true client pattern cannot help but emerge.

Part III asks, how can problem patterns be decoded? It looks at different models of therapy and at the basic ways in which they work: 'uncleanly', 'cleanly', directly, and indirectly.

Uncleanly

Here is one way of trying to decode client pattern:

> *Client These circles remind me of trying to use a compass as a child.*
>
> Therapist Yes, becoming independent of mother and finding your own way in the world can be very difficult.

We have been interpreting client information since long before Freud. How readily we translate it into patterns that relate to our own. "You'll see them as if painted in purple!" says psychotherapist Penny Tompkins. A therapist with an unresolved issue around their mother, say, might quickly pick up on a pattern that seems to be about the client's mother, but Clean Language only gives the therapist licence to use the word 'mother' if the client themself has used the word. The client in the example on page 31 has not used the word 'mother', but the therapist has. The client's mother now takes their attention, whether she deserves to or not.

Cleanly

A Clean facilitator's personal patterns might well affect the patterns they notice in others, but a genuinely Clean question will only reference information that the client has actually presented. In the early stages of a facilitative process, all information is treated equally.[2]

> Facilitator   And circles remind you of trying to use a compass as a child .. [Imagines client's family as having dysfunctional sense of direction, but sticks to Clean Language] and when trying to use a compass as a child, what kind of compass could that compass be?
>
> *Client The sort you draw circles with. I stabbed myself with the point and had to go into hospital.*

Not quite what the facilitator imagined. Approaching all client statements without presumption minimizes the impact of a natural tendency to speculate based on our experience of similar problems in ourselves and others. It also relieves us of responsibility for making 'meaning' of what we hear. Too often, a therapist will want to solve the mystery before they are halfway through the book.

Clean questioning is directed at the client's information, not directly at the client. This is a crucial difference between Clean and conventional questioning. Our preferences as Clean Language facilitators – a particular interest in family dynamics, say, or an eagerness to identify a client's resources – may influence the direction of our questioning, but if our questions are Clean, they will never be wholly irrelevant. The least they will do is facilitate the client to discover more about the particular aspect of the pattern that we have chosen to interrogate.

Who, then, is leading the therapeutic dance, client or facilitator? The facilitator may take the initiative with an opening question (typically "What would you like to have happen?"), but this is not in itself a leading question. It makes no assumption other than that the client has come for *something*.

Alternatively, the client may make the first move ("I'm going round in circles"), in which case the facilitator's follow-up question ("What kind of circles?" or "Is there anything else about going round?") immediately reflects the lead role back to the client. A synergetic sequence unfolds:

> client initial information ...
> *informs*
> therapist response-question ...
> *which prompts*
> client response-information ...
> *which informs*
> therapist response-question ...
> *which prompts*
> client response-information ...

The question of who is leading whom does not arise in a Clean exchange. It is the information manifested by the client that leads.

> Colin *I'll be going along quite happily and suddenly, wham, I'm doing the same old thing again, my head is spinning, I'm on a rollercoaster and there's like a big black vortex that sweeps me up off the ground and I have no control. I'm terrified, I'm very confused.*

Going along ... wham ... head spinning ... rollercoaster ... vortex ... what is this client's unconscious communicating? These metaphors are isomorphic (correspond in form) with internal patterns, but the language is cryptic, the information is in code. Would it be easier to decipher if the client were more succinct?

> Colin (concludes) *I've been going round in circles for years.*

Still quite puzzling, but the client has progressed from several descriptions of the problem to a simple description of the *pattern*. It is at a higher logical level.

> Clean Language therapist And you've been going round in circles for years. And when you've been going round in circles for years, what kind of circles could those circles be?

> Colin *It's like I'm on a roundabout.*

Now what? Colin has discarded one dysfunctional pattern in favour of another and still has no control. Or has he? Never interpret, never presume.

> Therapist And is there anything else about that roundabout?

> Colin It's a magic roundabout.

In two Clean questions, the metaphor has transformed from implacably binding problem to potential resolution with infinite [magic] possibility.

There are two other basic ways in which models of therapy work.

Directly and indirectly

Some clients will express themselves (even) more circuitously than Colin. Below is a symbolic representation of a certain cryptic pattern. Imagine the client is saying something that as their facilitator you cannot understand. It might as well be in code.

> Client A_____
> $\quad\quad$ B C

The client is expressing a fragment of the pattern that brought them to you. It is the taster before the feast. The pattern is isomorphically present. But what kind of pattern could this be?

In Part I, we considered how all patterns manifest in space, time, and/or form. There are obvious *spatial* components here. A seems to be 'above' B in some way, and B is 'further on' a bit. Is that enough to decode it? We could hazard a guess – repressive parent, subordinate child desperate for autonomy … or perhaps as the client goes on, the pattern will become more apparent.

> Client A   E F   H I   K L M N_____
> $\quad\quad$ B C D   G   J   O P Q

We can see now that the client's pattern is continuing not only in space, but over *time*. If you had made an intervention based solely on its spatial components, you might well have been wide of the mark. The client is manifesting a particularly idiosyncratic pattern, though with no insight of their own into it, they might well go along with whatever you suppose it to mean. For a while. Before relapsing.

In fact, this arrangement of the Roman alphabet has a very simple code. It is a pattern in not only space and time, but also *form*.[3]

If you take this little puzzle as a metaphor for any client presentation, there might be information for you as a counsellor or coach in the way you approached it. Chances are that you postulated one or two theories quite early on and attempted to fit the pattern to them, discarding any parts that did not fit and holding on to those that did until the theory so completely fitted the pattern that it could not be anything else. In other words, you took an objective view of the evidence and confronted it directly. A scientific or systematic method.

Or perhaps you decided not to be enticed by the 'A/B' form in which the puzzle appeared and approached it obliquely instead. You detached yourself in some way, took a path of your own, and either through belief or fancy imagined that the solution would follow. You worked in an indirect way on the pattern from outside it. An intuitive approach.

Or perhaps you supposed some sort of affinity with the pattern. You sat with it as it unfolded in the way that Einstein imagined himself riding a beam of light in order to understand relativity. You worked directly or indirectly on the pattern from alongside it. An empathic position.

And maybe there is another way. What led you to try to solve it at all? I guess, like me, you made an assumption that that is what you *ought* to do. And now that you have the solution (page 44, note #3), how can you be sure it is the 'correct' one? What if this client's conundrum dates back to Egyptian hieroglyphs and Sumerian pictographs, and further back still to a time before writing?

If you simply allowed yourself to *accompany* this client's process, made no presumptions or pronouncements, assisting it only to know itself, you would be identifying *with* the pattern from *within* the pattern, privy to its inherent logic, respectful of its unique purpose, and the client who came up with it would eventually have all the information they needed to decode it for themself (if that is what they wished to do).

To summarize: we can predicate four ways of decoding patterns:

> working *directly* on the pattern from *outside* the pattern
> working *indirectly* on the pattern from *outside* the pattern
> working *in/directly* on the pattern from *alongside* the pattern
> working *directly with* the pattern from *within* the pattern.

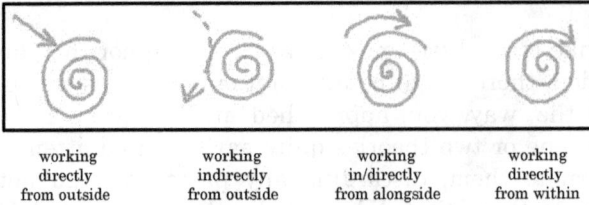

| working directly from outside | working indirectly from outside | working in/directly from alongside | working directly from within |

Figure 6 Four ways of decoding client pattern

Working directly on the pattern from outside

Client As I was saying, A _____ E ...
          B C D

> Traditional therapist (who might not even be thinking of the notion of 'pattern') I notice you have placed A and E above the line and B C D below, now I wonder what you make of that?

Most of the standard talking therapies – cognitive, client-centred, psychoanalytic, humanistic – might start in this way: aspiring to objectivity by remaining 'outside' the pattern. Yet if you analyze this intervention carefully, you will find that the therapist has introduced certain patterns of their own into the client's. "Placed", "above the line", and "below" are therapist metaphors. Too late. By now, the client has almost certainly incorporated them into their own process.

A Gestalt therapist might suggest confronting the parts of the pattern – placing A E F on one chair, B C D on another, and polarizing the disparity between them in the expectation of some sort of ideographical integration.

A transpersonal therapist might stress the spiritual dimension:

> Would you agree, A/B, that you are more than your appearance?

A transactional analyst might see the differences rooted in critical parent above the line and adaptive child below.

An existential therapist might focus on the 'givens' of human existence for A and B – death, alienation, and suffering – and then what?

A Freudian might check the information against a generalized model of transference and sexual development in order to help the client come to terms with its underlying pathological structure.

> I suggest to you that B really wishes to sleep with A, but
> must first kill C ...

Even a 'client-centred' Rogerian counsellor, wary of interpretation, attempting to reflect the client back to themself, would be predisposed in common with these other therapies to paraphrase the client's words and to install non-client material unwittingly.

> What you are saying is that B is playing low status in
> deference to A ...

In the traditional talking therapies, the therapist is in control of the process and interventions come from within the therapist's own patterns, personal and professional, self-derived and acquired. These may well include some eminently sensible perceptions and opinions, but also, inevitably, an irregular mish-mash of biases, whims, and weaknesses.

Here is an excerpt from a television documentary in which a (male) psychoanalyst is working with a (female) patient who suffers from so-called body dysmorphia. Diane is a pseudonym. She has been seeing the therapist for several months.[4]

> Therapist Good to see you again, Diane. How many hours a
> day would you say is spent thinking about your appearance
> now?

The therapist immediately sets the agenda for the session, characterizes the client's pattern, and ensures with the single word "now" that she is in it right away.

> *Diane Probably about six.*

The client has little choice but to respond in the therapist's limited (and limiting) terms.

> Therapist Six hours a day. So it's still ...

The key word "still" serves to anchor Diane to the problem pattern she has been in since she first came to see him.

> *Diane Yeh ...*

> Therapist Very significant.

> *Diane Yeh. It's a lot less. It used to be seventeen, maybe more.*
> *But within those six hours, a lot of that will be positive. I'll still*
> *be preoccupied, but I'll be thinking good things, just sort of how*
> *I'd like to have my hair next and that sort of thing.*

Diane is valiantly attempting to re-set the pattern and to re-model the therapist's position into something nearer her own.

> Therapist Uhuh.

> *Diane And also thinking about how I'm happy with my hair or how I'm happy with something I've got on.*

Diane is ready to find encouragement in anything, even that noncommittal "Uhuh" – which turns out not to be noncommittal at all:

> Therapist OK. I haven't seen that so often, where you're saying, you're saying it's not negative things, it's things where you're comfortable with.

Maybe because what she *is* saying is "thinking how I'm happy with my hair or with something I've got on." This information goes unacknowledged by the therapist, who seems to be committed to a pattern of his own.

> *Diane Yeh.*

Uncertain of her own perceptions, Diane is obliged to endorse the therapist's. Reassured by Diane's "Yeh", the therapist comes up with another theory.

> Therapist As if you're trying to reassure yourself.

> *Diane (pauses for several seconds) Yeh. Maybe. Yeh. Mm. Now you say that I don't know if it's such a good thing, but I was under the impression that that was all good. (Uncertain laugh) Even though I was still preoccupied, it was ...*

> Therapist Well it does suggest you're still quite vulnerable.

Whether she was before, she almost certainly is now and the chances are will continue to be for some time to come.

> *Diane Yeh. (Nods) Yeh. I suppose you're right.*

In the space of two minutes, the therapist has made three direct suggestions ("it's very significant," "you're trying to reassure yourself," "you're still quite vulnerable"), used one word of Diane's ("six") out of 131 possible, and placed her gently back in the unresourceful pattern that could keep her in therapy for years.[5]

I am not saying that this therapist was mistaken in his interpretation of Diane's pattern and clearly we don't know the full history of the therapy, but I do suggest that the language and the underlying methodology have as good a chance of being helpful to the client as the guesswork of the average clairvoyant. Not all talking therapies operate in this way. In cognitive-behavioural work, the interventions will be more structured. In humanistic therapies, they are often be more provocative. I have practised in both and I am not knocking either. Every methodology has its limitations, but every sort can be helpful for some.

Working indirectly on the pattern from outside

A way of working shared by the behavioural, physical, postural, sensory, expressive, and 'healing' therapies. I include homeopathy and traditional medicine among the physical therapies. I have worked in behavioural and expressive therapies. My knowledge of the others comes from experience as a patient and from family members who work in psychiatry and medicine.

Drug therapy supposes the body to be in a state of conflict with the patient's emotional and spiritual needs. Drugs work on the brain in the hope of indirectly modifying patterns in the mind.

Patient A seems to have to go there, B there, I'm not sure where to put ...

Doctor It sounds as if you're depressed. I think we'll put you on a course of amitryptiline.

Patient I don't know, doctor, what do you recommend?

Doctor You can have an injection or take the pills.

Patient What kind of pills?

I have worked with many clients who were concurrently on drug therapy and my sense of the best drugs did for them was to dull the problem without getting anywhere near the underlying historical or biographical pattern that produced it. Dulling a problem is an understandable way of coping, but hardly a way of developing a patient's potential.

Body and postural therapies – acupuncture, massage, reflexology, Feldenkrais, etc. – all work to one degree or another from outside. They aim to relieve the symptoms of negative patterns – pain, tension, stress – through movement or manipulation, and to influence internal events indirectly through mind-body or 'energy' connections.

Behavioural approaches such as 'familiarisation', 'aversion', or 'flooding', where the client is gradually introduced to more and more of the phobic trigger, work in the belief that changing behaviour changes thinking changes feeling, an essentially indirect approach.

'Healers' believe that their power comes from 'God' or from 'universal psychic energies'. The healer is the indirect conduit and the patient the passive receiver of energy transmitted in some indeterminate way from one to the other. Again, an indirect effect.

Expressive therapies, including art, music, dance, primal therapy, and anger release, work at one stage or several stages removed from the pattern. They explore the expression of feeling and seek the liberation of something, usually a symptom rather than a cause. You could call it the hopeful domino theory of therapy – free one component and trust that the rest will follow.

Although most indirect, non-drug based therapies describe themselves as 'holistic' and chacterize the patient as a body-mind-spirit whole, they are in fact partial and work on the mind in a secondary way via posture, muscle tension, or 'energy lines'.

Working in/directly on the pattern from alongside

I count hypnotherapy and NLP (neuro linguistic programming) in this category and I have practised in both. The hypnotherapist and the NLP therapist lead the client through a process and from the client's point of view, the process may be entirely internal.

> Client *There's this A and this B and ...*
>
> Hypnotherapist And as you see A and B, and hear the sound of my voice, and as your breathing gets deeper, I want you to ...
>
> Client *[Shifts from A B C to] Z – Z – Z ...*

In hypnotherapy, all that is required of the client is to respond passively and positively to the direction of the therapist. Once in a trance state, what happens next depends on the suggestivity of the client and the resourcefulness of the therapist. The effectiveness of the work is based on the therapist-led re-creation of generalized client resources which are brought to bear on the problem pattern obliquely.

The neurolinguistic (NLP) model says that our subjective experience is coded in sub-modality distinctions in the sensory cortex of the brain. Problem patterns thus have a coherent structure. Once the client has access to the structure, it can be described and decoded. And if that is done in the context of a well-formed outcome for change, change will happen.

> *Client I want to get rid of A.*
>
> NLP therapist And what will that get for you?
>
> *Client I'll feel better about B.*
>
> NLP therapist Okay, and what will that get for you?
>
> *Client What do you mean?*
>
> NLP therapist [tries another tack] When you say 'A' do you get a picture, a sound, or a feeling? Is that in black and white or colour? Moving or still?

Information about client patterns comes from sensory representations elicited conversationally by the therapist and reported cognitively by the client. That is arguably direct information, but it cannot help but be modified by its dependence on the therapist's own (NLP and personal) patterns and on the client's translation of their internal experience into a language that the therapist will hopefully understand. Thus, the work remains generalized and takes place in the vicinity of the pattern at best. Excellent indirect or partial modelling of client patterns is possible with NLP techniques such as sensory calibration, sub-modality analysis, meta-programme elicitation, strategy sequencing, logical level differentiation, and meta-model questioning, all of which require exquisite attention on the part of the therapist to client process. However, every one of these procedures is of necessity therapist-led and will not all (or always) apply to the client sitting in front of you. And as most client changework that stems from NLP modelling depends on the therapist-determined superimposition of good feelings over bad so that the bad have less significance, the resulting *patterns* (particularly in the case of therapist metaphor and so-called 'sleight-of-mouth' reframes) are likely to derive more from the ingenuity of the therapist than from the singularity of the client.

In NLP therapy, the client's outcome is elicited and explored cognitively – that is, in a state dissociated from the internal pattern that produced the desire for the outcome.

Working directly with the pattern from within

Imagine you are a therapist from another planet. You know all about electro-magnetic waves, but have never experienced them as 'sunlight'. Yet sunlight seems to have enormous significance for your earthbound client. Now the extraordinary thing about Clean Language is that you need to know nothing about sunlight in order to help your client put it to transformative use.

The Clean questioning of client metaphor is a glorious resource for any therapist. It elicits information that derives from the client's unconscious directly. The therapist does not have to reconstruct, paraphrase, or even 'understand' this information, which eliminates the need for interpretation and counters the therapist's natural tendency to generalize, delete, and distort what they hear.

Client outcomes can be elicited cleanly in a variety of ways, but are normally explored, and always evolve, in a state related to the pattern's intrinsic need for self-resolution – that is, from within the pattern itself.

Clean therapist And what would you like to have happen?

Client To understand A.

Therapist And to understand A. And when to understand A, what kind of A could that A be?

Client It reminds me of the frame of an attic roof.

Therapist And is there anything else about the frame of an attic roof?

Client I remember being sent to the attic. I'm two or three and I'm terrified.

Therapist And when sent to the attic, and you're two or three and you're terrified, where is that terrified?

Client (pointing to their heart) Here.

Therapist (nods to where client has indicated) And here. And does terrified here have a size or a shape?

Client Yes. (Gestures) It's about this big.

Therapist And (references gesture) about this big. And when terrified here is about this big, that is terrified like what?

Client Oh, like a balloon about to burst.

Therapist And when oh like a balloon about to burst, what kind of balloon could that balloon be, *before* it was about to burst?

Client Well, it's beautiful, red, light, and firm, and I'm having fun with it.

Never-before-discerned patterns begin to emerge through Clean Language modelling as the therapist facilitates the client to identify component parts of their symbolic and metaphorical perceptions; to develop these components in form, space, or time; to elucidate key relationships between them; to discern patterns across the client's perception of those relationships; and to translate the relationship of those patterns to their everyday lives. As the client explores their perceptions in a state somewhere between trance and full awareness, they are in essence modelling themselves. It is the *client*, not the therapist, who determines the significance of their perceptions. And as the system learns about its own organization, a context for self-generated change is created, and it is the *client*, not the therapist, who determines what needs to happen for the system to evolve.

Summary

The table below summarizes these four direct and indirect approaches to decoding problem patterns.

THERAPY MODEL	METHODOLOGY	WHAT HAPPENS	RELATIONSHIP TO CLIENT PATTERN	'CLEAN'?
1 Cognitive Client-centred Humanistic Psychoanalytic Transpersonal Existential	Conversational, assumptive	Client talks. Therapist questions, interprets 'analyzes', suggests	Working more or less directly on the pattern from outside the pattern	NO
2 Behavioural Postural Massage Medicine Acupuncture Homeopathy 'Healing' Expressive therapies	Mostly nonverbal, intuitive	Client receives or expresses. Therapist does, 'senses', might teach, might prescribe	Working indirectly on the pattern from outside the pattern	NO
3 Hypnotherapy NLP	Internal, 'empathic'	Client internalizes. Therapist elicits, leads	Working in/directly on the pattern from alongside the pattern	NO
4 Clean Language Autogenic Metaphor Symbolic Modelling Clean Space The Power of Six	Verbal, nonverbal, internal	Client talks, does, internalizes, expresses. Therapist listens, watches, questions, accompanies	Working directly with the pattern from within the pattern	YES

In my own practice, I find Clean models of facilitation to be as respectful as client-centred counselling, as inner-resourceful as hypnotherapy, as modelling-efficient as NLP, and as liberating as any humanistic intervention. They can be as spiritually integrative as transpersonal therapy, as expressive as art therapy, and as systematic and rigorous as psychoanalysis. They are without doubt holistic, in that all parts of the client are engaged, intimately connected, and explicable only in reference to the whole.[6]

Colin has decoded his problem pattern. The information is intelligible. Is that enough?

₪

Notes to Part III

1 A code is a system of words or signals used for other words or signals to achieve brevity or secrecy. 'Decoding' was Grove's metaphor for deciphering/unscrambling/figuring out the pattern that the client's words, gestures, moves, and drawings represent. If decoding suits/pleases/resonates with you as a metaphor, good/okay/fine, otherwise do substitute your own.

2 In the early stages of a Clean process, all information is treated equally. At more advanced stages, some information is likely to be more equal than others.

3 Credit to Wendy Sullivan for introducing this A/BC pattern to our Clean Research Group and getting us (eventually) to decode it. The letters above the line have only straight lines; the letters below have curved lines.

4 Diane and the analyst sequence adapted from a longer deconstruction in *Trust Me, I'm The Patient*, pages 45-48. The therapist here had been chosen to represent the work of a respected body of British analysts, so we may assume that the process with Diane was subject to both his and the organization's approval at both rough-cut and final stages of editing.

5 Psychoanalysis and psychodynamic counseling, with their emphasis on conscious insight by the client, might be the comparatively prolonged procedures they are because neural connections from the cortex (the 'seat of reason') to the amygdala (the 'emotional processor') have been shown to be less numerous than those from the amygdala to the cortex. This might explain why it is easier for emotion to govern reason than the other way round. Joseph Ledoux, *The Emotional Brain*, op. cit.

6 For more on the various Clean models of inquiry, see cleanlanguage.co.uk, powersofsix.com, and wayfinderpress.co.uk

Part IV
How Can the Information Within
a Pattern be Released?
disengaged / liberated / freed

Since all symbols have attributes, and all attributes have functions, and all functions serve a purpose, all symbols are potentially useful somewhere, somewhen, or under some conditions. Lawley and Tompkins

Discernment and decoding of internal patterns is just that. Nothing will change as a result until the client is able to put personal meaning to the information that their unconscious has scrambled, compacted, unpacked, and revealed. As clients begin to make sense of the information, they discover what their symbols signify and become aware of a different kind of internal processing. This can be a defining moment. And it is at this moment – when the system recognizes its own organization, when internal intention is revealed, when conscious and unconscious knowing come together – that the information in the pattern is released.

How can a facilitator facilitate release? After all, if the liberation of information from what had hitherto been a conservative (self-preserving) pattern were a predictable and logical process, all a person would need would be a well-meaning friend to point out the obvious. Given that most of us require something more than a well-meaning friend to bring about change, let alone deep structural change, is there a formula that will work for any Clean facilitator with any client under practically any conditions?

The answer, surprisingly, is yes. Before I share this formula with you, please read the following oath:

I shall not attempt to change, resolve, or reconfigure the client's problem pattern. I shall not guess what needs to happen for the pattern to change, resolve, or reconfigure. I shall only seek to encourage the conditions for the client to change, resolve, or reconfigure the pattern in their own way.

Here are four basic ways to facilitate the release of information in a pattern and to encourage the conditions for change *if the client so chooses.*

1 ASK POTENTIAL RESOURCE SYMBOLS FOR THEIR INTENTION AND FOR WHAT NEEDS TO HAPPEN FOR THAT INTENTION TO BE FULFILLED

> Colin *It's a magic roundabout.*
>
> Clean therapist And it's a magic roundabout. And when it's a magic roundabout, is there anything the magic of that roundabout would like to do?

There is no supposition in the construction of a Clean question like this that "magic" is necessarily good or bad, or that it can change "roundabout" or anything else for better or worse. There is, of course, a hint in the word itself that 'magic' might achieve anything the owner wishes. Otherwise, the intervention simply acknowledges that magic exists as a symbol in the metaphor landscape, confirms that it has been constructed as a modifier, and draws attention in non-specific terms to its potential.

> Colin *Magic would like to change the circles the roundabout has been going round in for years to spirals that keep developing without repeating themselves.*

"Would like to change" is an interesting pointer to change, but in itself is going nowhere.

> Therapist And *can* magic change the circles ...?

The client, having articulated the intention of the symbol, is invited to consider if the intention can be fulfilled.

> Colin *With the right input of energy at the right moment, yes.*

All symbols have resource potential. A resource symbol might at a given moment be overt and self-evident ('*magic*', '*love*', '*sunlight*', etc.), or latent ('*roundabout*', '*years*', '*spiral*') and require interaction with another symbol, or to be put to work in another context, before it is able, as David Grove would say, "to confess its strengths."

Resources can come to light in unlikely places. One of my clients transformed a 30-year pattern of addiction after finding a redemptive gem in a metaphorical garbage can. Others have found energy for resolution or healing in kittens, sunflower seeds, and the far reaches of the cosmos. Identifying and activating potential resource symbols is one considerable way in which the information within a pattern can be released.

2 FOCUS THE CLIENT'S ATTENTION ON THE PATTERN

This might mean persisting with Clean Language beyond the call of duty.

> *I've been going round in circles for years.*

> And you've been going round in circles for years. And you've been going round in circles for years ...

Such is the reiterative power of this first, reflective, phase of the syntax that Colin now has unequivocal affirmation of his pattern and has almost certainly been associating back into it.

> And when you've been going round in circles for years ...

What next? Once a pattern has been brought to the client's attention in this way, almost any Clean question will do. There might be valuable information in Colin's "circles" or "years", or even in his "going round".

> ... what kind of going round could that going round be?

> *Colin Clockwise.*

New information. We could simply affirm it and return to the client's original metaphor, or concentrate his attention on this promising development. Remember that all patterns manifest in space, time, and/or form. A basic spatial question will allow Colin to discover if he has embodied this aspect of the original pattern, or if he can locate it in the perceptual space around him.

> And where could clockwise be?'

> *Here. In my heart.*

> And whereabouts in your heart?

> *(Gestures to centre) Right here.*

Everything has to be somewhere. Knowing *precisely* where a pattern or part-pattern is located in the body or the surrounding landscape is a prerequisite for getting to know it better and discovering more about it.

And when clockwise is right here in your heart, what time could it be?

Oh, time to stop blaming myself.

We could equally have drawn Colin's attention to the indirect indicator – the homonym – in "clockwise".

And what kind of wise could the wise of that clockwise be?

It knows more than I do.

And when it knows more than you do, what does it know?

A question that could take both client and facilitator into the world of 'Emergent Knowledge'.[1]

And what else does it know? ... And what else? ...

Colin has an opportunity while going round in clockwise circles to focus on what he wants rather than what has been holding him back. If his (internal) clock knows more than he does, it could be invited to come up with a solution. Colin would have found an indirect way out of his repetitive circles of inaction.

Any one of these approaches to focusing – checking out potential resource symbols, drawing attention to the pattern as an entity, zeroing in on certain symbols, words, and part-patterns – could provide the key to unlocking the pattern and releasing the information therein. Colin must first confirm and reconfirm to himself that going round in circles represents the core problem he must address. The pattern will thereafter be more amenable to giving up what only it knows.

3 DRAW ATTENTION TO THE WIDER CONTEXT IN WHICH THE PATTERN APPEARS

Colin I've been going round in circles for years.

We could invite Colin to see the bigger picture. *'How does going round in circles relate to X or Y ?'* (Something else in the client's life or landscape that he has identified.) Or we could invite him to explore the wider space-time parameters within which his pattern appears.

And when going round in circles *then what happens*?

I feel stuck.

And when you feel stuck, then what happens?

The circles stop.

And when circles stop, then what happens?

I'm stuck.

And when stuck, then what happens?

It starts all over again.

Colin now knows that going round in circles leaves him feeling stuck, which stops the circles, which leaves him feeling stuck again, which sets him going round in circles again until he stops again. A self-sustaining sequence that seems to be going nowhere, but Colin has actually identified a strategy. Once identified, a strategy, however repetitive, however persistent, can be revised. Here is one question that will help:

> And stuck ... and stuck ... and when stuck, *what happens just before* it starts all over again?

The question invites Colin to momentarily 'freeze' a moment between what had previously felt like two inextricably conjoined events ("stuck" and "starts all over again") and to consider what might be happening in that micro-moment.

> *I feel very young and stupid.*

A fleeting bodybrain event, in all probability related to a memory of trauma. In the normal run of events, a feeling like this will happen too quickly to notice or be given credence. Now it can have the attention ("Where could feel very young and stupid come from?" etc.) it almost certainly deserves. If the feeling is healed, it will no longer prompt stuckness. If stuckness doesn't happen, the pattern will have transformed.

Another wider context question is *'How do you know?'*

> And when you're stuck, *how do you know* you're stuck?
>
> *I feel heavy and hopeless.*

Colin has given himself permission to acknowledge an associated feeling, an embodied way into the pattern. The question might also allow him to notice something else that is going on concurrently.

> And when you're stuck, *how do you know* you're stuck?
>
> *Everything around me is moving.*

We might even ask:

And when going round in circles, then stop, then stuck, then starts all over again ... *what is beyond?*

A distant rainbow.

Every pattern is part of a bigger pattern. Every bigger pattern offers an opportunity for finding a more powerful, inclusive resource that can be taken back to bear on the original problem.

4 GIVE CREATIVE ASSIGNMENTS

The client can be encouraged to explore the pattern in a variety of other ways — by mapping its key features on the flipchart; by physicalizing it in space; by researching the etymology of a word or the cultural history of a symbol; or by any creative means feasible. It was not until Colin drew the sequencing of his stuckness on paper and gave his once-ideational notion a graphical equivalent that he discovered a number of new places be could explore:

just before stuck ... /

during stuck / ... /

between stuck and circles / ... /

just before circles ... /
during circles / ... /
between circles and stop / ... /

during stop / ... /

between stop and stuck /... /

I have been witness to a thousand ways in which clients have used mapping to reveal new information. Any one of these space/times might yield a resource or the impetus for doing something differently, or for moving on in a new way.

Today a client admitted to feeling what she called "anger" in her relationship with her partner. She was concerned. I invited her to represent the problem on the flipchart. Rather than drawing a symbol (red mist, clenched fist, etc.), she simply wrote out the word 'anger', then stood back, studied it for a moment, and said:

Oh. I've used lower-case letters, and I've written it in black.
I thought it would come out in capitals, and be red and
dramatic, this is old anger, I know why it's there.

Discerning and decoding her anger in her own way – not the therapist's – allowed this client conscious insight into her current state, obliged her to own it and move on. I am reminded again to cherish the unique creativity of every individual.

In Part I, we distinguished pattern from non-pattern. Part II considered various credible and less credible ways of discerning pattern – association, implication, focusing on the foreground, background, and so on. Part III looked at ways in which problem patterns can be decoded: cleanly, uncleanly, directly, and indirectly. Part IV examined the role of Clean Language and Autogenic Metaphor in releasing information held in the pattern.

What happens when this information is released? Resolution is not always a straightforward affair. What exactly is the nature of change? How can facilitators encourage the conditions for change in the final stage of this five-part process?

₪

Note to Part IV

1 'What do you know?' 'And what else do you know?' See *The Power of Six* for a full set of 'Emergent Knowledge' questions and an explanation of the Emergent Knowledge process. The questions will also be found in Appendix C of *Trust Me, I'm The Patient*.

Part V
Then What Happens?
The Nature of Change

When the information in a pattern is released, things change. The result will be reassignment, rearrangement, translation, or transformation.

Reassignment

With reassignment, *one or more elements in the metaphor landscape reorganizes to modify its form or function, but the underlying pattern stays the same.* The system remains in self-preservation mode. It might even shift its organization sideways so as not to change. Colin gets to know a little more about his circles, but life goes on pretty much the same.

Rearrangement

With rearrangement, *elements in the metaphor landscape reorganize their relationship to each other, but the underlying pattern stays the same.* Colin feels a little differently in his circles, he finds himself going round in a slightly different way, he experiences some insight into the effects of his going round, but he is not yet ready to change the essential going roundness of his system.

Reassignment and rearrangement generally mean having to go round the therapeutic/developmental loop again. My job as facilitator is to continue drawing Colin's attention to any part of his pattern which has the potential for change (which might be any part); to facilitate him to move elements forward in time to see what happens; and to invite him to consider how the relationships between elements might evolve.

Translation

In 'translation', *the pattern changes, but its underlying structure stays the same.* This might suffice for a while. Some people find it agreeable enough to continue in the old pattern with new awareness. It frees them to explain their behaviour to themselves, to adapt temporarily to it, or to make a conscious effort to find out more about it. As integral philosopher Ken Wilber says:

> *Translation itself is an absolutely necessary and crucial function for the greater part of our lives. Those who cannot translate adequately fall quickly into severe neurosis or even psychosis.* (*The Essential Ken Wilber*, Shambala 1998)

Time spent adapting to a pattern or experiencing it differently might seem fruitless, but can be productive. Clients will use the time to explore hitherto unexplored patterns with more understanding. Some find themselves better able to recognize when they are in and not in the pattern, which gives them space to compare its benefits and disbenefits.

Colin hopes that his new awareness will be enough for the old pattern to transform spontaneously without further ado, but instead it reappears in another guise. His persistent circles convert into uncertain spirals. "Things are on the up for a week or two," he tells me, "then they collapse and I'm going nowhere again." He is disappointed to experience no fundamental change in his core sense of himself. Ken Wilber again:

> *At some time in our maturation process, translation itself, no matter how adequate or confident, simply ceases to console.*

Rather than continuing to ride his symbolic spirals upwards and outwards into thin air, Colin finds himself adapting them into the form of a rotary drill, which he directs downwards into the earth. He creates a tunnel that takes him back through the landscape of his life to the terrain he inherited. As a child, he suffered frequent and regular abuse in the family. He developed a capacity for emotional dissociation which helped him survive, but there was a price to pay. Dissociation led to isolation, isolation to depression, a pattern that became habitual (circular) and inhibitory.

As Colin decodes the meaning in his metaphor, his perspective on the past changes and he considers for the first time the possibility of real change in himself. He makes adjustments in his responses to the world. The cycles of anxiety appear less frequently. They are more predictable and less distressing.

With many clients, conversion of this kind is acceptable for a while. Colin will decide in his own time if and when he is ready to make more fundamental and far-reaching change. Meanwhile I can direct his attention to the smaller changes he has already made and invite him to extend their potential.

Transformation

In this state of grace, *the nature and structure of the pattern changes radically or completely*. Rather than the pattern modifying as a result of the client self-modelling, it metamorphoses. There is a pronounced difference in its condition or character. The initial mutation might itself be quite small, but properly noted, coaxed, and supported ("And then what happens?" etc.), it will have a progressive effect.

> *When a symbol changes, it not only alters itself, it is likely to influence other symbols. If enough changes occur, or a change of sufficient significance occurs, the client's symbolic perceptions reorganize and a transformed metaphor landscape emerges.* Lawley and Tompkins

What results is a qualitatively new pattern of organization. The tadpole becomes a frog; the caterpillar a chrysalis; the chrysalis a butterfly. New choices emerge and a new way of being begins.

Transformation can be sudden and spontaneous, or it can happen gradually or cumulatively.

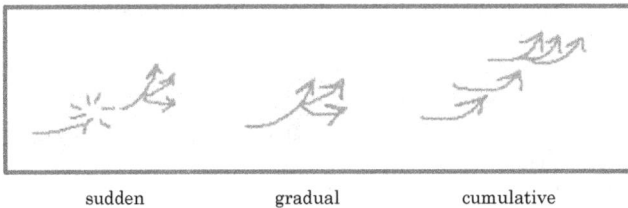

| sudden | gradual | cumulative |

Figure 7 Three kinds of transformation and the emergence of choice

One client used his rapid resolution of what had been a disabling fear of the dark as the catalyst for resolving his relationship with his mother en route to a gradual change in his whole sense of himself. A client with arachnophobia (and a raft of unwanted behaviours, feelings, and beliefs associated with it) chose to tackle her patterns the other way round – by first resolving a childhood trauma that had no obvious connection to the phobia.

Both clients experienced the effect as cumulative – increasing the energy for resolution through successive additions.

Resolution

The complete pattern resolution process is summarized below.

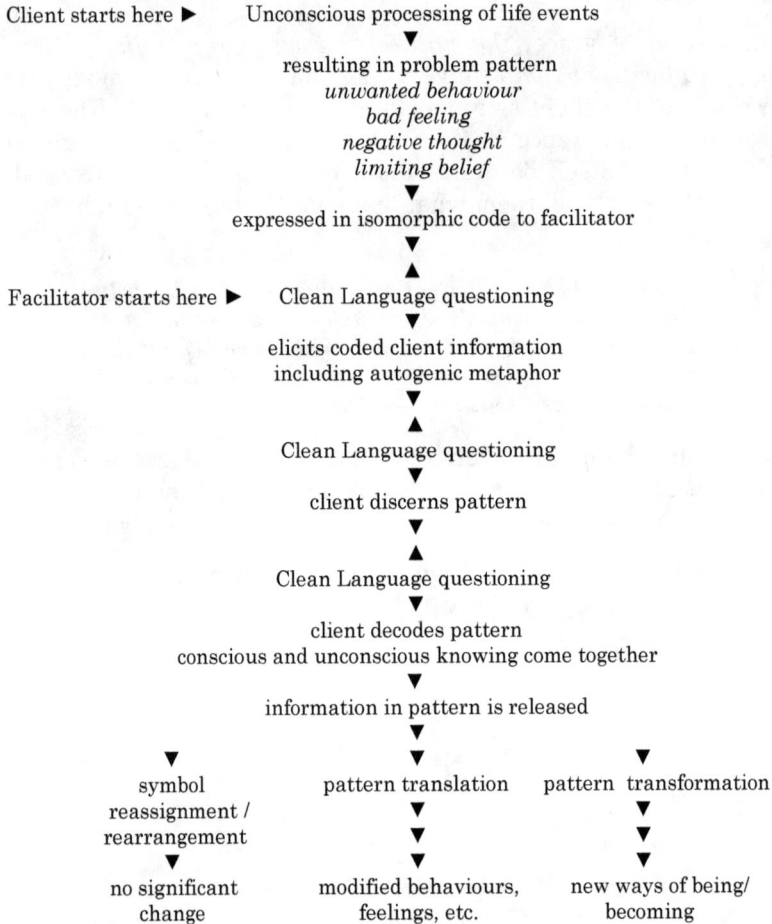

Client starts here ▶   Unconscious processing of life events
▼

resulting in problem pattern
unwanted behaviour
bad feeling
negative thought
limiting belief
▼

expressed in isomorphic code to facilitator
▼
▲

Facilitator starts here ▶   Clean Language questioning
▼

elicits coded client information
including autogenic metaphor
▼
▲

Clean Language questioning
▼

client discerns pattern
▼
▲

Clean Language questioning
▼

client decodes pattern
conscious and unconscious knowing come together
▼

information in pattern is released
▼

▼	▼	▼
symbol reassignment / rearrangement	pattern translation	pattern transformation
▼	▼	▼
▼	▼	▼
no significant change	modified behaviours, feelings, etc.	new ways of being/ becoming

A member of the Clean Research Group came to the seminar we held on 'Pattern' unprepared. Normally this colleague is very well prepared: a familiar, productive, self-affirming pattern. On this particular day, he gave a presentation on what it was like in the time leading up to the seminar to have consciously changed the habit of a lifetime. He felt nervous and uncomfortable, unable to anticipate what would happen and aware of an almost irresistible pull to revert to the habit of having something prepared – that is, to relapse.

Many clients report similar feelings when they make significant change. Old patterns offered advantage and revising or losing them might not always bestow immediate or evident benefit. An addictive client explained to me that his dependency habit was like going down a familiar road, it supposed a kind of mobility, whereas the prospect of change was like arriving at a junction where there were too many exits and not enough signposts, a paradoxical situation in which he felt he could only progress by standing still. He needed to discover more about the destination before he would commit to the journey. Other clients realize that they have changed only after feedback from others who knew them well. And some will change a pattern and forget they ever had a problem.

How Clean Language works

What clients for Clean Language have in common is a commitment to themselves that stems from the knowledge that the changes they make are theirs and *theirs alone*. They have not been devised or directed by the therapist. I believe this fosters a more organic, lasting, and reliable resolution.

As a reflective methodology, Clean Language pays immaculate attention to the systemic, self-referential nature of problem patterns. Systems theory describes the output of a system re-entering the system as new input to influence the next output. What Clean Language does is enhance/concentrate/deepen the quality of the facilitator's input, which in turn enhances/concentrates/deepens the value of the ensuing client output.

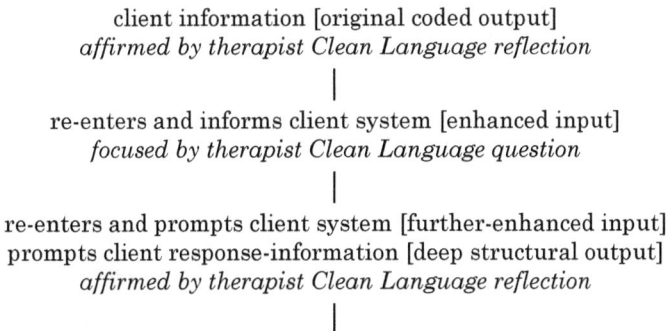

client information [original coded output]
affirmed by therapist Clean Language reflection

|

re-enters and informs client system [enhanced input]
focused by therapist Clean Language question

|

re-enters and prompts client system [further-enhanced input]
prompts client response-information [deep structural output]
affirmed by therapist Clean Language reflection

|

|

re-enters and prompts client system [still-further-enhanced input]
focused by therapist Clean Language question

|

re-enters and informs client system [still-further-enhanced input]
prompts client response-information [deeper-structural output]
affirmed ... (etc.)

In Part III, we raised the question of who is leading whom in a Clean Language exchange, facilitator or client? In fact, it is the *information* manifested by the client and affirmed, focused, and activated by Clean questioning that self-energizes the system and keeps it updated. And as the unproductive pattern in the system is detected and decoded ... as the information is released and the pattern translates or transforms ... the system is no longer subject to self-delusion and new, more productive patterns can form.

And what happened to Colin? At first, his circles translated into longer, more purposeful loops as he began to notice more of what was going on around him. After a while, they transformed into creative spirals whose energy propelled him into a spacetime where he could become more the person he wanted to be. Today he is an educational psychologist and counsellor facilitating others to discern, decode, and resolve their personal and group-related patterns. You might say he has come full circle.

Acknowledgments

My co-researchers for the Clean and Emergent Research Group seminar on 'Pattern' were Clive Bach, James Lawley, Frances Prestidge, Sheila Stokes, Wendy Sullivan, and Penny Tompkins.

Thanks to Carol Thompson for her suggestions.

Rapport, the journal of the UK Association for NLP, and the cleanlanguage.co.uk website were the original publishers of the articles on which this paper is based.

Author

Philip Harland is a psychotherapist specialising in Clean Language, Autogenic Metaphor, and Emergent Knowledge. He trained in analytic, humanistic, and neuro-linguistic psychotherapies and worked closely over many years with David Grove, the originator of Clean Language and Emergent Knowledge.

More books by Philip Harland

Trust Me, I'm The Patient
Clean Language, Metaphor, and the New Psychology of Change

The Power Of Six
A Six Part Guide to Self Knowledge

How The Brain Feels
Working with Emotion and Cognition

Possession And Desire
Working with Addiction, Compulsion, and Dependency

www.wayfinderpress.co.uk